Easy & Elegant Quilts

by Sara Nephew

Dedication

To my daughter Elizabeth, who lent her artistic skills to the creation of this book.

Acknowledgements

Sincere thanks to:

Annette Austin, Diane Coombs, Pamela Foster, Jean Look-Krishano, Marjorie Lorant, Bonnie Mitchell, Betty Parks, Mary Ferguson-Pierce, Kathleen Springer, and Lynn Williams for pattern testing.

Annette Austin, Pat Beck, Nadine Darby, Rose Herrera, Judy Eide, Beverly Payne, Helen Whitaker, and Penny Wolf for their beautiful machine or hand quilting.

Credits

Photography by Carl Murray
Graphics by Elizabeth Nephew
Cover by Jean Streinz

All quilts in this book have been designed, pieced, and quilted by Sara Nephew unless otherwise noted.

Easy & Elegant Quilts

Printed in the United States of America.

Clearview Triangle

8311 180th St. S.E.
Snohomish, WA 98290
USA

Library of Congress Card Number 93-72737
ISBN 0-9621172-3-4

Contents

Preface

As a result of having written a number of quilt books, I've been lucky enough to be asked to teach and to demonstrate my rotary cutting methods many times. Often as I cut a shape, I would say," You could make a whole quilt out of this shape..." Saying it got me thinking about what quilts could be made out of the shapes I cut. So this book originally was about quilts that are made completely from one shape, the *one-patch* quilt.

The shapes that interest me are 60° shapes. The potential for new quilt designs is great, and rotary methods have made these shapes easier to cut than ever before. Also I think 60° designs have an elegant difference, a flavor of the unusual, that draws me back to them.

Introduction

This book has been planned for ease of use. As in my previous books, to save space and eliminate repetition, a separate section of cutting directions precedes the quilt patterns. If you do not know how to cut a particular shape, just flip back to the cutting section. With these simpler quilts, I have kept the cutting section simpler also. Instead of including every element of my method, suitable for even advanced quilt designers, only the shapes needed for each quilt in the book are explained. You may wish to skim through this section first, or just turn to a pattern and begin. An index at the back will help you find particular cutting directions.

The quilts are generally organized in order, with the easiest pattern at the beginning and the most challenging patterns at the back of the book.

A Charming History

One-patch quilts have a venerable history. Many of the earliest hand-pieced quilts consisted of one shape, like the hexagon or the 60° diamond, with the design then formed by the arrangement of colors or dark or light fabrics in the quilt top (*Mosaic, Grandmother's Flower Garden, Tumbling Blocks*). English quilt pieces were often basted over paper shapes and the shapes hand stitched edge to edge (paper piecing). All quilts were hand pieced until the invention of the sewing machine, and many unusual shapes were tried.

One-patch quilts were the basis for a fad near the end of the 1800's. Many quilters tried piecing a *Beggar's Quilt*, also called a *Charm Quilt*. This kind of quilt is a game a quilter can play. The aim is to make a quilt of many pieces with each piece a different fabric. Some unmarried young girls aimed for a quilt of 999 pieces. If more pieces were accidentally included, the superstitious said the girl would remain unmarried. Sometimes two pieces in the whole quilt would be identical, thus including another game of finding the two identical pieces of fabric in the quilt. The Charm quilt has had a new popularity in recent times, and ads can be found in quilting magazines offering to exchange pieces of fabric with anyone in the world. Ladies have been known to cut sections out of the inside yoke of their husbands shirts to satisfy their collectors' instincts.

A modern game often played with the one-patch quilt is to use the simple format as a showcase for something special done with fabric. The quilter may have a collection of unusual fabrics, perhaps collected during trips to other countries, (or purchased at the quilt shop of her dreams). Or she may want to stretch her knowledge of color and design. In either case the simplicity of the one-patch quilt allows concentration on the design characteristics of the fabric. Often the quilter is able then to produce a quilt that is beautiful indeed, a step beyond previous results.

One-Patch or Two

A beginning quilter often tries a one-patch pattern first, because it looks easy enough. Just cut out lots of one shape and sew them together. A machine piecer may find this simple logic presenting some problems. A hexagon, for example, pieced by machine, is a challenge even for an advanced quilter in the sheer number of set-in seams. And sewing together 60° diamonds into the *Tumbling Blocks* pattern has been abandoned in the middle many times, with the quilt top consigned to the garage sale or worse. Most of the quilt designs given here are pieced with all straight seams. Sometimes the pattern has more than one shape to avoid set-in seams. Only three quilts still have set-in seams, and in each case these are a third or less of the total seams in the quilt. These three patterns were more attractive and less bulky if a few seams were set in.

Another unexpected challenge of a one-patch quilt is the irregular edge that often is the result of an unusual shape. In the past, quilters have responded to this challenge in three ways: they bound the edge as is, with its changing angles; they appliquéed the irregular edge to another straight piece of fabric (sometimes using this as a border); or they trimmed the edge straight with a scissors or rotary cutter.

The quilt directions in this book finish the edge a fourth way. Shapes are cut that fill in the irregularities around the edge, and these are pieced into the quilt top. Then the top is ready for the addition of borders or binding with straight edges and without losing seam allowances.

Pressing Tips

The quilter who has not previously worked with 60° angle quilts will become aware of some additional bulk in seam intersections. This is because six or more seams are coming together instead of the familiar four. To reduce this bulk, try using a dry iron to press until one block is completed. Then wet a piece of old cotton sheet or muslin and lay it over the completed block. Run the iron over it, remove the wet press cloth and dry the block with the iron. The wet press cloth is a tailoring technique that gently flattens the block, minimizing any bulk.

Occasionally you may wish to allow a seam to twist along its length so the seam intersections on either end can be pressed in the direction that produces minimum bulk. Plan a quilting pattern that will avoid the seams.

About Borders

Many of the quilt samples in this book are finished with a border fabric that is not included in the body of the quilt itself. The important thing is to find the perfect fabric to make the quilt glow, to bring out and strengthen the important elements of the quilt design. Whether or not the fabric *matches* anything in the quilt is not the most important consideration. So even though the fabric requirements in each pattern give yardage needed for the border, you may wish to purchase this fabric after the majority of the quilt top is complete.

Always measure the finished top at both side edges and in the center to find the average measurement for the border in one direction. Then pin the centers of both the top and border. (For a larger quilt, centers and quarters may be pinned.) Ease the border on. After both side borders are on, measure the new width of the quilt at two edges and in the center to find the average measurement for the two remaining borders and seam them on the same way.

Games to Play

My intention is not to do a dissertation on color or art theory, but to suggest a few enjoyable design strategies that could make these simple quilts even more fun to make. Think of it as being armed with a list of ingredients in your favorite store (the fabric store, of course). Then vary the ingredients to your taste. At the beginning of marriage, I made up my mind to learn how to cook a lemon meringue pie. It must have taken five or six pies until a smooth, fluffy lemon pie resulted. But neither of us complained about the tasty lumps in the other pies! They were yummy and fun to make.

We are learning with every quilt we make, also. And each one is a pleasure to make and use. Try a fabric game for the fun and satisfaction you will receive in the delightful flavor of the finished product.

Your ingredients are: color, value, pattern, texture, and line.

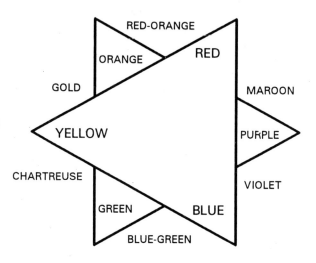

1.The basic colors are called "primary" or "secondary". The primary colors are the simple colors of the rainbow, with no other colors mixed in-pure color. There are three primary colors; red, yellow, and blue.

The secondary colors are found where the primary colors blend into each other. Red plus yellow creates orange, red plus blue makes purple, and blue plus yellow results in green. All additional colors result from various mixes of the primary and secondary colors.

2. Value is the lightness or darkness of a color. White is as light as you can get, black is the darkest dark, and everything else is a tint or a shade in between. A quilter must use fabrics of different value for the quilt design to show.

3. Pattern or texture is usually obtained by using printed fabrics. A solid fabric is plain and serene, while a print is busy and causes your eye to move over the fabric surface.

4. Line is an element of a quilt pattern when plaids and striped fabrics are inserted. This is fun to try.

EYE FOR DESIGN

As you piece your quilt, lay the blocks out where you can begin to judge the elements of design and color you are working with. Add or subtract fabric pieces and rearrange blocks until the quilt pleases you. This is a very exciting process and has many elements of meditation involved. After working for a few hours, it feels like coming down to earth to answer the phone or stop to make supper. If you hit a snag, persist in trying to get it right. Take a break to rest as necessary, ask for suggestions, but try to achieve the beautiful quilt you see in your mind's eye.

THE CHARM QUILT:GAME #1

This old-time quilt game is still popular with modern quilters. The rule is to have all the pieces of fabric in the quilt be different. Any pattern can be used, but the one-patch type of quilt lend itself well to such a mixed color scheme. Fabrics may be purchased, traded with friends, cut from old clothing, or whatever. Even though this is a very random multi-colored design, care must still be taken with fabric choices and color placement to achieve a pleasing effect. This could be a very long-term project.

Variation: Plan for exactly two pieces of fabric in the quilt to be the same, so another, smaller game is included in the quilt.

COLOR PLAY:GAME #2

MONOCHROMATIC

Fabric selection is based on shades and tints of one color. At the fabric store, choose one major color and look for pastels, brights, and deep darks of this same color. How many fabrics can you find? Don't forget black and white as choices. You may wish to choose solids, tiny prints, and big bold prints to mix. *Be sure to include both light and dark fabrics so your quilt will have an effective design.*

Variation #1: Add one bright accent of another color.

Variation #2: Widen your color definition a bit to include slightly changing hues. For example, if the color is red, let yourself mix reds with a little blue cast , pure scarlets, and reds with more orange in them, in all shades and tints.

Variation #3: Use many large prints for a different look (adding pattern or texture).

COLOR PLAY:GAME #3

PRIMARY

All three of the primary colors--red, yellow, and blue--work well with each other. Any two or three are a good combination. Use them pure and strong for a bold or childlike effect. Add white or black for a background color.

Variation #1: Use tints of primary colors in combination. Pink and pale blue, for example, are a favorite color scheme of quilters. Make sure to add a darker or lighter color to create an effective quilt design.

Variation #2: Use a dark shade of a primary color with one or two of the other primaries. Maroon with clear blue or navy with bright red are common. What about bright red and yellow with navy? Can you make it work? Does adding white or black make a difference?

COLOR PLAY:GAME #4

ANALOGOUS

This selection method involves choosing related colors to combine. At the fabric store, choose one primary color (red, yellow, or blue) plus the two secondary colors that are close to the chosen color. So, for example, if the primary color chosen is blue, then one additional fabric will be blue plus red (purple) and the remaining fabric will be blue plus yellow (green). You may also choose to include the hues between the primary and the secondary colors, blue-purple and blue-green. These are all colors that are next to each other on a color chart. Choose fabrics while being sensitive to your feelings about the color combinations. Remember to include light and dark colors so your quilt design shows.

Variation #1: Add a bright accent of another primary or secondary color.

Variation #2: Choose one secondary color (orange, purple, green) and the two primary colors it is made from.

Variation #3: Instead of just three fabrics, choose many fabrics with subtle color and value changes to use in your quilt design.

COLOR PLAY:GAME #5

COMPLEMENTARY

This approach to color chooses a primary plus the secondary color that results from mixing together the other two primary colors. (These colors are always opposite each other on a color chart.) These are traditional color schemes for many uses, and are very satisfying.

Your fabric choices are: red and green, blue and orange, or yellow and purple.

Don't forget that you need some light fabric and some dark fabric. Respect your feelings and intuitions as you choose your fabric.

Variation #1: Add an accent of another color.

Variation #2: Try looking at cool and warm variations of one or both of the two complementary colors. Lay them out in combination at the fabric store. Take what you like, leave what you don't.

COLOR PLAY:GAME #6

MULTI-COLORED

This color scheme uses all the primary and secondary colors. Choose red, yellow, blue, green, purple, and orange fabrics. Brown, white, and black can be added to these colors. *It is not necessary that these colors all be used in equal amounts!* This can be surprisingly successful in a quilt.

VALUE RANGE:GAME #7

Choose any color scheme of two <u>or more</u> colors. Then find each color in four <u>or more</u> values from light to dark. Carefully arrange the cut fabric pieces of your quilt pattern to shade from light to dark in part or all of your quilt design.

Variation: Choose light, medium, and dark fabrics, and arrange them so the quilt pattern shows an illusion of 3-D.

TEXTURE:GAME #8

PAINT WITH PRINTS

Choose at least 10 different printed fabrics, small and medium prints. The busy qualities of these prints should have the same effect as many small brush strokes by a skilled painter. Be sure some of the chosen fabrics are dark, and some light, so the quilt design will show.

Variation: Remove all texture from the quilt by working with solids, so only the changing colors of the individual fabric pieces cause your eye to move over the quilt.

PATTERN:GAME #9

DESIGN WITHIN DESIGN

Choose a large print with a repeat. Cut out the repeat section carefully so that the turning angles of the quilt pieces, or your careful positioning, forms a new secondary design.

LINE:GAME #10

RHYTHM AND REPEAT

Choose linear fabrics like plaids and stripes and cut these carefully so that the lines play across the surface of the quilt design. Group linear repeats for emphasis and arrange the lines carefully for balance. Let your eye see the shapes formed as lines cross. Are they large or small, light or heavy?

Variation: Look for fabrics with lines of different widths (bold, heavy, narrow, fine) and character (smooth, ragged, continuous, broken) and try them in combination.

FABRIC DESIGN:GAME #11

Produce your own fabric by sewing strips together, doing crazy patch, sewing tucks for surface texture, or any fabric manipulation. Then cut your pattern pieces from your changed fabric.

Variation: Dye, print, or paint plain or printed fabric. Many techniques exist for changing fabrics with your own skills.

Rotary Cutting Tools

Rotary cutting all the shapes in these quilts is one of the techniques that make the designs easy. The quilts go together more quickly than you would expect. Two key tools save time when making these quilts. The **Clearview Triangle** makes accurate rotary cutting of 60° triangles, 60° diamonds, hexagons, etc., fast and easy. The triangle comes in three sizes. The **Half-Diamond** speeds the cutting of some additional shapes. These tools are made from ⅛" acrylic, for use with a rotary cutter. (See pg. 64 for ordering information.)

Besides **Clearview Triangles**, required tools are: a rotary cutter, a cutting mat, and a clear, straight ruler like the Salem Rule or Omnigrid (for cutting strips). A large rotary cutter is preferred, since it saves muscle strain, cuts faster, and tends to stay on a straight line. I also like a ruler that measures 6"x12" for cutting strips. The shorter rule is less likely to move during cutting.

Shapes To Cut

Cutting Strips

The first step in cutting any shape is cutting a strip. All fabric should be prewashed. 100 percent cotton is preferred.

1. Fold fabric selvage to selvage and press. Bring fold to selvage (folding again) and press.

2. Use a wide ruler as a right angle guide, or line up the selvages with the edge of the mat, and the ruler with the mat edge perpendicular to the selvage. Cut off the ragged or irregular edges of the fabric.

3. Cut the strip width required, using the newly cut fabric edge as a guide.

NOTE: Directions are given in the patterns for the width of strip to cut for each shape required.

To cut **triangles**:

1. Cut a strip according to the pattern directions. Put the top point of the **Clearview Triangle** at one edge of the strip and the measurement required in the pattern at the other edge. *A triangle is cut from a strip whose width is the height of the triangle.*

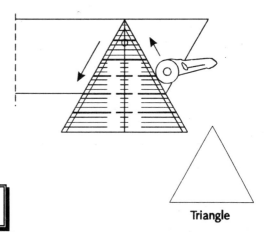

Triangle

Triangle

2. Rotary cut along the two sides of the triangle. Then move the **Clearview Triangle** left or right along the same edge (do not flip it to the other side of the fabric strip) for the next cut. Line up the tool at the point and the fabric edge again.

3. Cut along both sides of the triangle.

> **TIP** Strips may be stacked up to six thicknesses and all cut at once.

To sandwich piece **matching triangles**:

1. Cut strips of fabric the width required in the pattern. Two different fabrics are used, often one light and one dark. Seam these strips right sides together with a ¼" seam down both the right and the left side of the pair of strips.

Matching Triangle

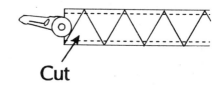

Cut

2. Cut triangles from the stacked and seamed set of strips. Pull the tips of the seamed triangles apart and press the seam to the dark.

To cut a **diamond**:

1. Cut a strip the width required in the pattern. Place one side of a **Clearview Triangle** along one edge of the strip. Cut the end of the strip to a 60° angle.

2. Turn the **Clearview Triangle** so the tip is at one edge of the strip and the required measurement at the other edge. Rotary cut **only** the side away from the first cut.

3. Keep moving the tool along the same side of the strip, lining it up and cutting along the side away from the first cut.

TIP Strips may be stacked up to six thicknesses and all cut at once.

To cut a **quarter hex**:

1. Cut a strip and cut rectangles according to pattern directions or according to the table below.

2. Position the **Clearview Triangle** with one side along the long edge of the rectangle. Cut the end of the rectangle to a 60° angle.

Triangle Size	Strip Width	Rectangle
2"	1¾"	2⅛"
3"	2¾"	3⅜"
4"	3¾"	4½"
5"	4¾"	5⅝"
6"	5¾"	6⅞"

Tip Quarter hexes do have a reverse of their shape, so check the diagram to see which direction to cut the 60° angle.

To cut a **long diamond**:

1. Cut a strip the width required in the pattern. Trim one end of the strip to a 60° angle.

2. Place the **Clearview Triangle** over the fabric strip, setting the bottom edge of the strip at the measurement given for the long diamond in the pattern. Cut only the side away from the first cut.

Tip Long diamonds do have a reverse shape, so check to see which angle is needed before you cut.

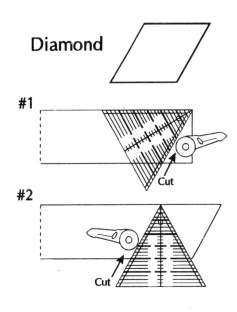

Diamond

#1

Cut

#2

Cut

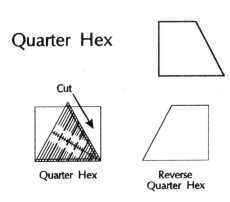

Quarter Hex

Cut

Quarter Hex

Reverse Quarter Hex

Long Diamond

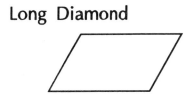

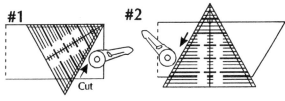

#1

Cut

#2

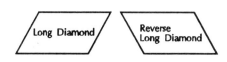

Long Diamond

Reverse Long Diamond

To cut a **flat pyramid**:

1. Cut a strip the width required in the pattern.

2. Place the **Clearview Triangle** over the fabric strip, lining up the bottom edge of the strip at the measurement given in the pattern. Rotary cut along both sides of the triangle. Turn the tool to the other edge of the strip, line it up, and cut again.

To cut a **triangle half**:
Method #1

1. Cut a strip the width given in the pattern. Cut triangles from the strip.

2. Place the **Clearview Triangle** over the fabric triangle with the center line of the tool along one edge of the fabric triangle. Rotary cut along the edge of the tool that is centered on the fabric triangle. This produces a left and right triangle half.

OR: Method #2

Cut a rectangle according to the measurements given in the pattern. Lay the edge of a ruler from corner to corner as indicated in the pattern and rotary cut. This will give you two triangle halves exactly alike.

To cut the **teardrop shape**:
Method #1

1. Cut a strip according to the measurement given in the pattern. Cut triangles from this strip.

2. Position the **Clearview Half-diamond** over the fabric triangle upside-down. Make sure the top point of the fabric triangle is under the center line of the tool, the pointed tip of the tool is just at the bottom edge of the fabric triangle, and the triangle sides are lined up evenly with one of the rulings (see diagram). Then use the rotary cutter to trim away the two excess points.

OR: Method #2

1. Cut triangles as #1 above.

2. Place the center line of the **Clearview Triangle** along the base of the fabric triangle, with the point at the center. Rotary cut this wedge off. Reverse the tool and cut off the other corner wedge.

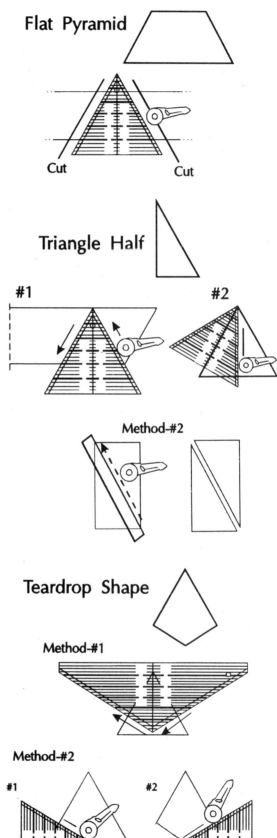

To cut a **diamond half**:

Method #1

Use the **Clearview Half-diamond** to rotary cut 120° triangles from the proper width strips as given in the pattern.

OR: Method #2

1. Line up the center line of the **Clearview Triangle** with the edge of the proper width strip. Rotary cut along one edge of the triangle.

2. Turn the tool, line up the center line at the edge of the strip and rotary cut the other side of the diamond half.

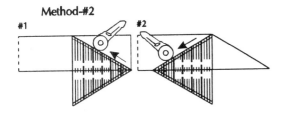

Method-#2

#1   #2

To cut a **hexagon**:

1. Cut diamonds from the strip width required by the pattern.

2. Then cut a triangle from both ends of each diamond that is half of what the strip width was.

To cut the **gem shape**:

1. Cut diamonds from the strip required by the pattern.

2. Then cut a triangle from one end of the diamond that is half of what the strip width was.

To cut the **long hex**:

1. Cut a long diamond from the strip required by the pattern, at the proper line on the **Clearview Triangle**.

2. Then cut a triangle from each end of the long diamond that is half of what the strip width was.

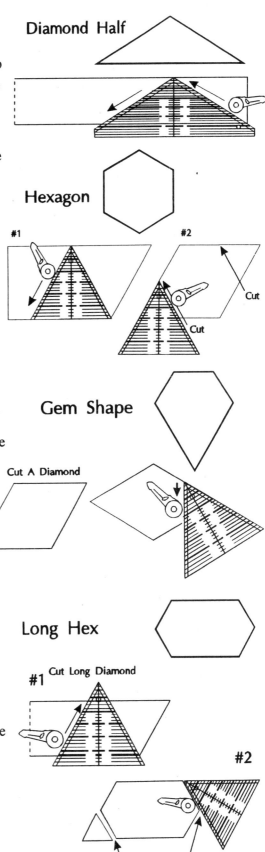

Diamond Half

Hexagon

#1   #2

Cut

Cut

Gem Shape

Cut A Diamond

Long Hex

#1   Cut Long Diamond

#2

Cut Off Triangles

Using These Patterns

Welcome to 15 quilt patterns for rotary cutting. As you are cutting and piecing, if you need a reminder of how to cut a particular shape, turn to pgs.10-13 or check the index in the back of the book for page numbers for each shape. Soon you will be putting beautiful quilts together. The patterns are generally arranged in order from the very easiest to the more challenging. Pick one that looks like fun to you and begin!

PAPER LANTERN WALL HANGING

4" triangle size
Wall hanging with border: 29" x 33"

All fabrics at least 45" wide prewashed.
Fabric Requirements:
12 fat quarters of busy florals
½ yd. border fabric

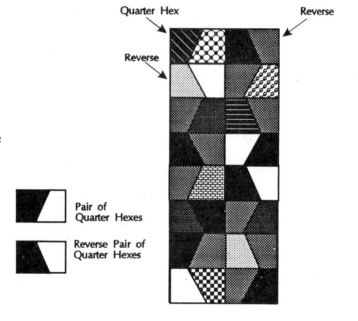

Directions:
1. Cut 64 fabric rectangles 3¾" x 4½".
Place the Clearview Triangle along one side of the fabric rectangle as shown on pg. 11 and trim one end to a 60° angle. Trim the rectangles right sides together to get the angle and its reverse. Cut 32 quarter hexes and 32 reverse quarter hexes.(see diagram)

2. Sew two quarter hexes together as in the diagrams at right. Sew 16 pairs and 16 reverse pairs of quarter hexes. These are rectangles again.

TIP A ¼" fabric triangle will stick out on each side. The seam falls in the notch.

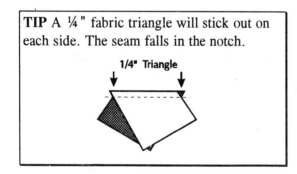

Paper Lantern Wall Hanging

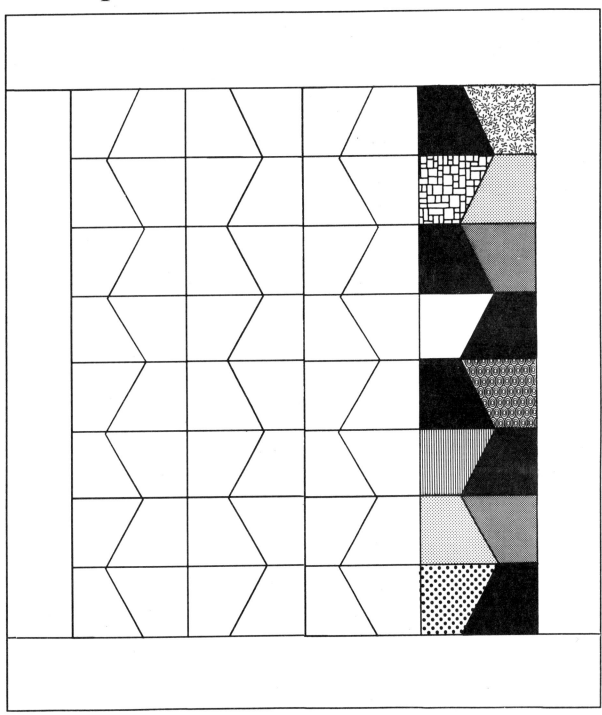

3. Sew the 32 seamed rectangles in four vertical rows. Begin rows one and three with quarter hexes and rows two and four with reverse quarter hexes. Also alternate quarter hexes and the reverse as you piece each vertical row. Lay out the pieces to form light and dark lantern shapes.

4. Sew the rows together. Add a 3¾" border.

TIP Press seams up in the first and third row and down in the second and fourth row. The seams will butt for accurate piecing.

Press Up row 2 Press Up row 4

row 1   Press Down   row 3   Press Down

PAPER LANTERN QUILT

5" triangle size
Quilt with border: 77¾" x 86½"

All fabrics at least 45" wide prewashed.
Fabric Requirements:
12 or more ⅓ yd. pieces of batiks, large oriental prints, etc.
2¼ yds. border fabric

Directions:
1. Cut 256 fabric rectangles 4¾"x 5⅝".

2. Continue as in Paper Lanter Wall Hanging above. Make four wall hangings and sew them together. Add a 9¼" border.

Paper Lantern, 29" x 33". An assortment of Liberty of London fabrics paints color and texture into this simple pattern. Even though lighter or darker fabrics can be placed randomly, careful arrangement of the pieces will cause hexagons to emerge from the busy floral background.

Paper Lantern, 77¾" x 86½". A collection of Kimono fabrics and other Japanese prints, Dutch Java prints, batiks, and American printed fabrics are combined in this quilt for a sophisticated look. The author enlarged the scale of the pattern to complement the large prints of many of the fabrics. The top was pieced in four sections and then combined. Quilted by Rose Herrera.

Herringbone Braid, 51½" x 58¼". Red, yellow, and blue with a strong accent of dark green combine in this graphic quilt. It would be easy to make a larger quilt by making longer braids, perhaps even with strips between the braids. Pieced and machine quilted by Annette Austin.

Bubbles, 53" x 61½". Busy floral prints combine to suggest the hint of a landscape to the imagination. Pink touches in the blue fabrics warm and soften the scene. Pieced by Diane Coombs and quilted by Judy Eide.

Facets, 25½" x 28¾". The use of light, medium, and dark fabrics creates a 3-D illusion in this design, even though no consistent color or value placement is required. Using a range of values in a design always adds a glow, a radiance to the finished quilt. Pieced by Mary Ferguson-Pierce and quilted by Rose Herrera.

Triangle Sparkle, 54½" x 64½". This combination of prints and colors suggests the smoke and embers of a warm winter fireplace in a darkened cabin. It would be good to wrap up in and sit by a fire. Quilted by Beverly Payne.

Ribbon Pinwheel, 47¾" x 65¼". The pink, yellow, and blue pinwheels make this quilt look like it has been tied up with ribbons. Blending floral backgrounds and pastels produce a soft, pretty coverlet that is just perfect for a granddaughter. Pieced by Pamela Foster and quilted by Helen Whitaker.

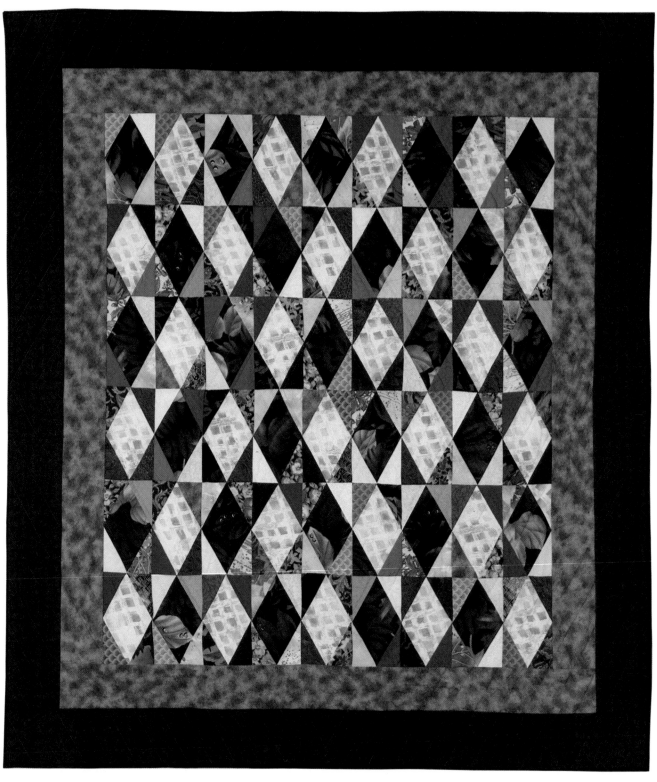

Old-Fashioned Diamond, 49¼" x 54". Do you see the stars in this sparkling quilt? Mirrors, windows, and cut crystal are suggested by the crisp points and diamonds highlighted by dark and light fabrics. Pieced by Jean Look-Krishano and quilted by Nadine Darby.

OLD-FASHIONED DIAMOND

4" triangle size
Quilt with borders: 49¼" x 54"

All fabrics at least 45" wide prewashed.
Fabric Requirements:
Choose an assortment of seven or more
colors, both light and dark, ⅓ yd. each
½ yd. inner border fabric
1 yd. outer border fabric

Directions:
1. Cut 12 selvage to selvage assorted strips
of fabric 2⅝" wide. Sew the strips right
sides together in pairs with a ¼" seam down
both sides. Cut the sewn sets of strips into
forty-eight 4½" sections as shown.

2. Place the Clearview Triangle over one cut
section with the center line of the tool along
one long fabric edge and the 4½" line at the
bottom short edge. Rotary cut as shown.
Turn and check the other side of the
rectangle for accuracy. Trim as necessary.
Pull the cut half-triangles apart at the tips
and press the seam to the dark. Seams may
need to be flipped later to make them butt.
You should have 96 half-triangles.

TIP Flip some of the sections over before
cutting to produce both left and right half-
triangles as shown.

Half-Triangle

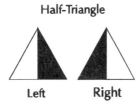

Left   Right

---

3. Cut seven strips 3¾" wide in an
assortment of colors. Cut diamonds from
these strips. You will need 54 diamonds.

4. Using one diamond and two half-
triangles, make one *Old-fashioned Diamond*
block. Make 42 blocks altogether.

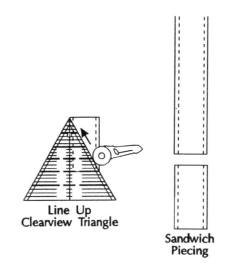

Line Up
Clearview Triangle

Sandwich
Piecing

Old-Fashioned Diamond Blocks

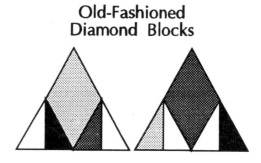

5. Cut a selvage to selvage 2⅝" strip from one light and one dark fabric. Cut 4½" rectangles from each strip. Bisect the rectangles diagonally using the Clearview Triangle for accuracy as in #2. Cut 24 triangle halves. Cut 12 left and 12 right.

6. Using one diamond, one half-triangle, and two triangle halves, assemble a right or left finishing piece. Make six left finishing pieces and six right finishing pieces.

7. Sew seven complete blocks and a right and left finishing piece into a horizontal row. Make six rows. Sew the rows together. Add a 3¾" inner border and a 4½" outer border.

TIP To produce a quilt measuring 68" x 77½" without borders multiply the fabric requirements by four and make four quilt tops as above. Then sew them together as shown.

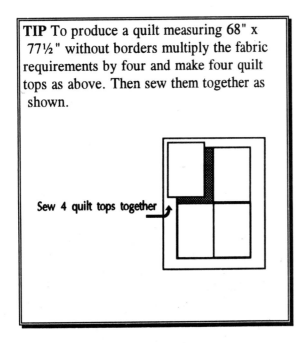

Sew 4 quilt tops together

Finishing Pieces

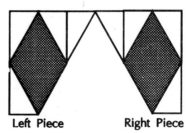

Left Piece   Right Piece

Cut Fabric
Strips

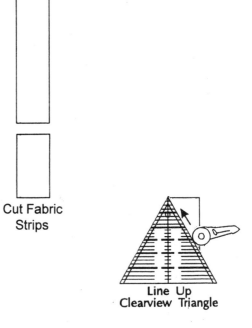

Line Up
Clearview Triangle

Or Flip Rectangles Over

Old-Fashioned Diamond

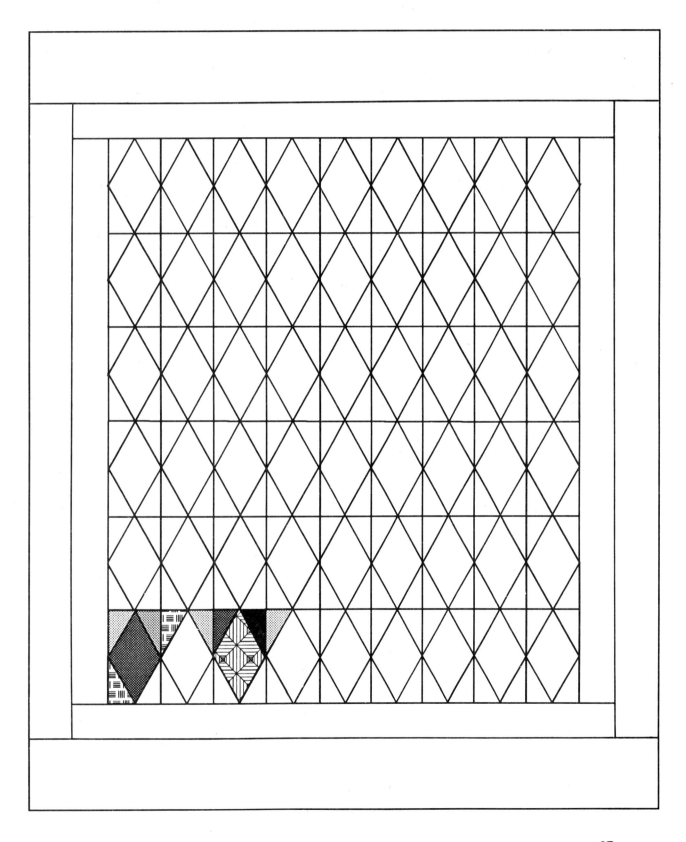

BUBBLES

4" triangle size
Quilt with borders: 53" x 61½"

All fabrics at least 45" wide prewashed.
Fabric Requirements:
¼ yd. each of eight different fabrics
½ yd. inner border fabric
1 yd. outer border fabric

Directions:
1. Cut 96 flat pyramids from 3¾" strips of fabric at 7¼" on the Clearview Triangle.

2. Sew eight flat pyramids together in a vertical strip as shown. Finish the ends of rows top and bottom with 4½" triangle halves cut from 4½" triangles. Make six rows like this. Make six more rows with the flat pyramids in the opposite direction.

3. Sew rows together in pairs of opposites. Then sew the six pairs together to make the quilt top. Add a 2¼" inner border and a 5½" final outer border.

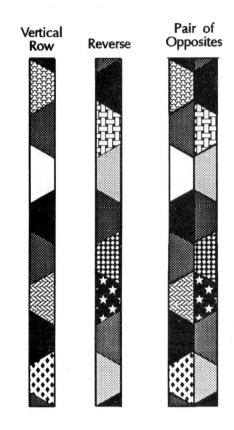

Vertical Row   Reverse   Pair of Opposites

TIP Offset the ends so ¼" triangle sticks out on each side. The seam falls in the notch.

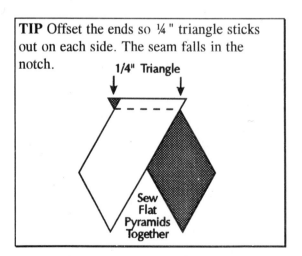

1/4" Triangle

Sew Flat Pyramids Together

Bubbles

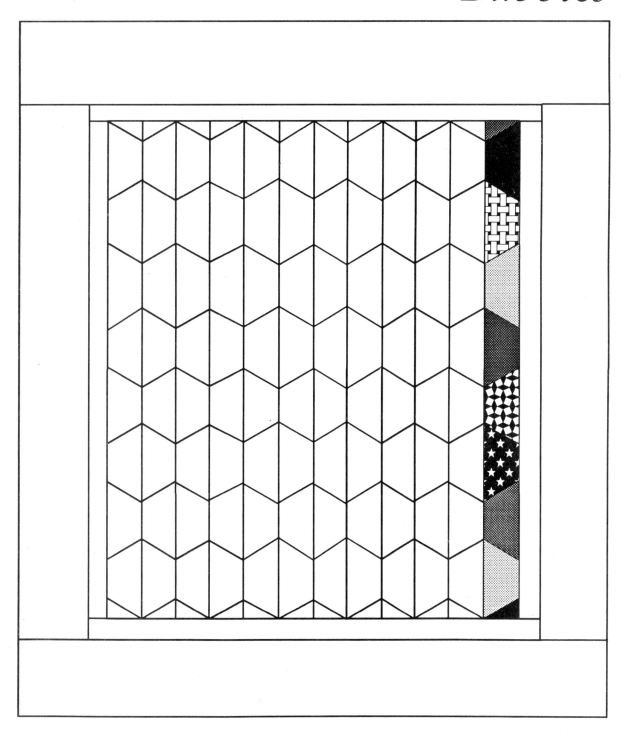

HERRINGBONE BRAID

4" triangle size
Quilt with border: 51½" x 58¼"

All fabrics at least 45" wide prewashed.
Fabric Requirements:
¼ yd. of eight or more different fabrics (or fifteen 3¾" different colored fabric strips from prewashed fabric)
¼ yd. of background fabric
1¼ yds. border fabric

Directions:

1. Cut four diamond halves from a 4¼" strip of background fabric. Cut 88 flat pyramids from 3¾" strips at the 7¼" line on the Clearview Triangle.

2. Sew a flat pyramid to the <u>right</u> side of a diamond half.

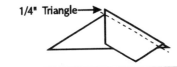

TIP A ¼" triangle of the flat pyramid should stick out past the center angle of the diamond half. The seam falls in this notch.

1/4" Triangle→

3. Then sew the next flat pyramid to the other side of the diamond half and the short end of the flat pyramid as shown. Keep sewing the flat pyramids to alternate sides of the braid until 22 are sewn on.

4. Trim off the excess part of the diamond half even with the edge of the braid. Begin sewing the next braid with the flat pyramid on the <u>left</u> side of the diamond half.

5. Finish the top of each braid with a 4½" and 11" triangle half cut from 4½" and 11" triangles. You will need four of each. Sew the vertical braids together and add a 6½" border.

1.

Diamond Half

2.

First Flat Pyramid
Started on the Right Side

First Braid Alternate Braid

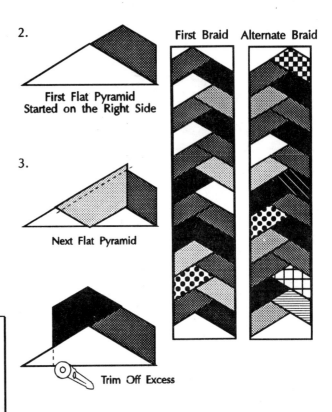

3.

Next Flat Pyramid

Trim Off Excess

TIP As the flat pyramids are sewn on, press the seams of the flat pyramids on the left side, up, and the seams of the flat pyramids on the right side, down. Then when the braids are sewn together, all these seams will butt up against each other.

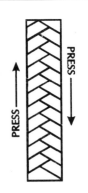

PRESS

PRESS

Herringbone Braid

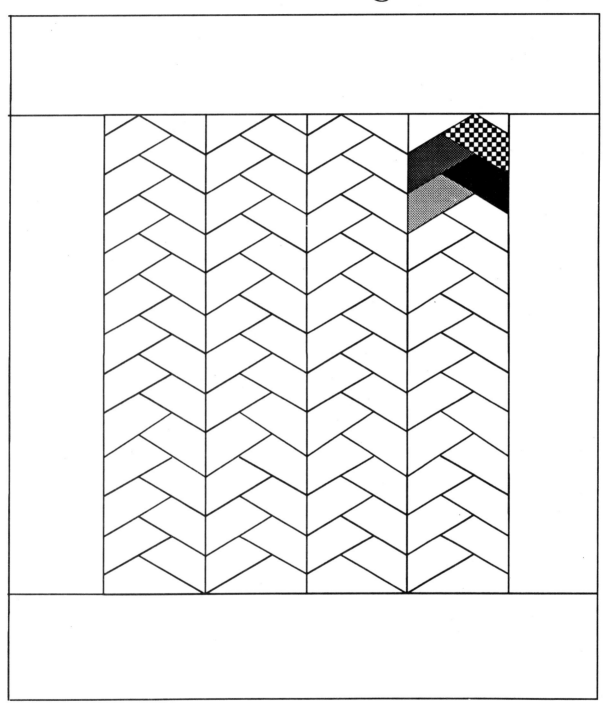

TRIANGLE SPARKLE

4" triangle size
Quilt with border: 54½" x 64½"

All fabric at least 45" wide prewashed.
Fabric requirements:
⅓ yd. of five different fabrics
¼ yd. of 13 more fabrics
1½ yds. of border fabric

Directions:

1. Cut twenty 4" selvage to selvage strips of fabric. Use a mix of different colors. From these strips, cut 320 triangles (4").
Or:
Sew two 4" strips of fabric right sides together with a ¼" seam down <u>both</u> sides. Cut matching triangles from the seamed sets.

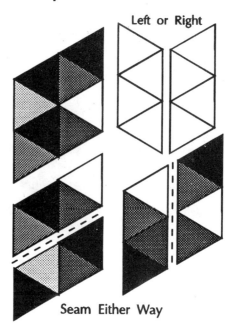

Sparkle Block

Left or Right

Seam Either Way

Matching Triangle

Pull apart at the tips and press seams to the dark. You will need 160 matching triangle units.

2. From four matching triangle units, construct one block. Mix the colors. Make 40 blocks altogether.

3. Cut assorted 4" triangles from scraps of the other fabrics, or take apart any extra matching pairs. Cut 16 triangles altogether. Cut 16 diamond halves from two 2⅜" strips. Sew 4" triangles to them to make fill-in pieces as shown.

Fill-in Piece

4. Sew five blocks and two fill-in pieces into a horizontal row. Make eight horizontal rows. Sew these rows together as in the quilt diagram. Add a 6½" border.

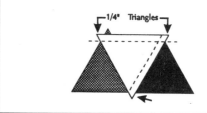

TIP Offset the pair of matching triangles so there is a ¼" triangle of fabric sticking out at each side. The seam falls in the notch.

¼" Triangles

COLOR TIP Plan for a cool set of blocks and a warm set of blocks so the colors can change from one end of the quilt to the other. Make about 30 blocks at random and then begin to lay out the quilt.

Horizontal Row

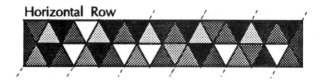

Triangle Sparkle

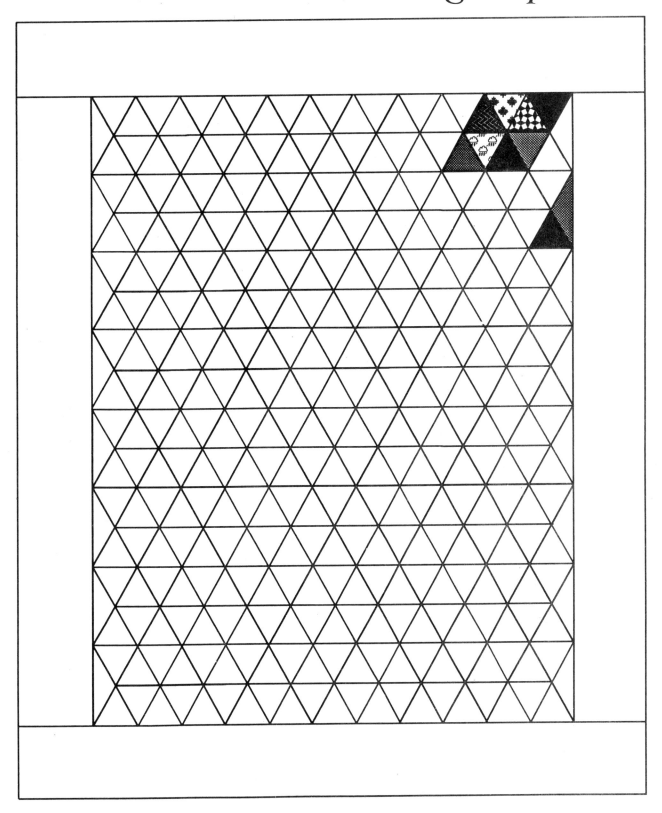

RIBBON PINWHEEL
SMALL QUILT

4" triangle size
Quilt with borders: 47¾" x 65¼"

All fabrics at least 45" wide prewashed.
Fabric Requirements:
2¼ yds. background print
assorted 2⅝" strips of pinwheel fabrics:
       1 dark blue, 1 yellow, 1 plain blue,
       1 plain pink, 1 pink print,
       1 blue print
½ yd. of second blue print
⅔ yd. border fabric

Directions:

1. Cut a 2⅝" strip of light background fabric and one of the pinwheel fabrics. Sew the strips right sides together with a ¼" seam down both sides. Make 10 sets of strips altogether. Cut the sewn sets of strips into 4½" sections as shown.

2. Place the Clearview Triangle over one cut section with the center line of the tool along one long fabric edge and the 4½" line at the bottom short edge. Rotary cut as shown. Turn and check the other side of the rectangle for accuracy. Trim as necessary. Pull the cut half-triangles apart at the tips and press the seam to the dark. Trim off the long seam ear at the top, back to a 60° triangle shape. You should have 90 half-triangles.

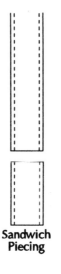

Half-Triangle

**Sandwich
Piecing**

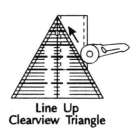

**Line Up
Clearview Triangle**

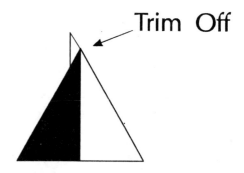

Trim Off

Ribbon Pinwheel

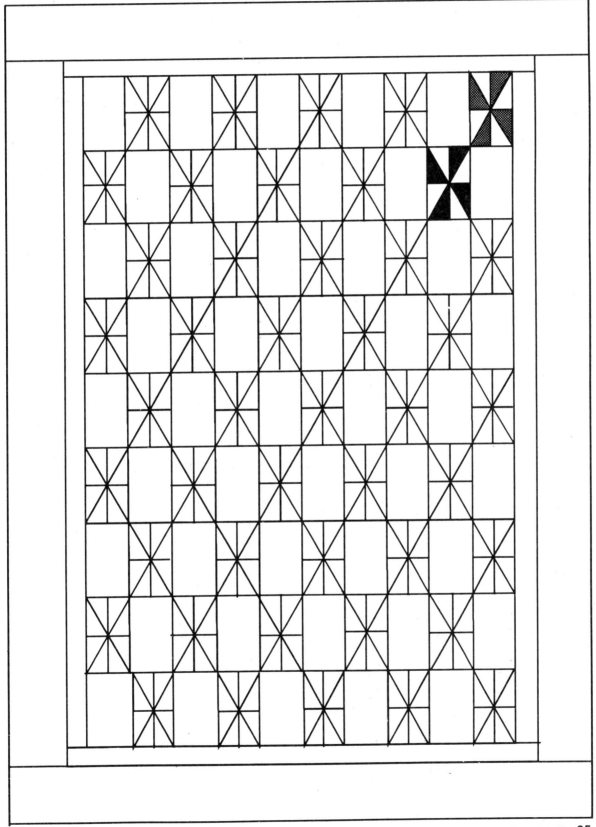

3. Cut another 10 sets of 2⅝" strips from background and pinwheel fabrics. DO NOT SEW SIDE SEAMS, but layer in sets.

Cut 2⅝" x 4½" rectangles as before. Then: Choose a pair of seamed half-triangle sets of the same color. Cut the rectangles diagonally as needed to produce the side triangle halves. (See the diagrams at right.) Cut the rectangles using the Clearview Triangle for accuracy as in #2.

Note: If you flip sections over to make the pinwheel turn the other way, make sure you flip two sections for a complete block.

Flip Set So Pinwheel Fabric Is Up

Flip Set So Background Fabric Is Up

4. Make one Ribbon Pinwheel half block by sewing a background and a pinwheel triangle half to one half-triangle as shown. Match the fabric pieces at the top of the triangle as shown in the diagrams. Make another half block the same way. Sew the two halves together according to the diagram. Make 45 complete blocks altogether.

 or

Half-block   Half-block

5. Cut 45 rectangles measuring 4¼" x 7" from light colored prints. (You may wish to measure your blocks and adjust this alternate block to match the average size of your blocks.)

6. Sew light print rectangles from #5 alternately with Ribbon Pinwheel blocks in rows according to the quilt diagram. Sew the rows together and add a 2" inner blue border and a 3½" outer print border.

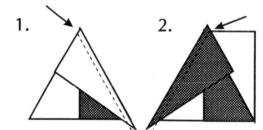

RIBBON PINWHEEL LARGE QUILT

4" triangle size
Quilt with borders: 96" x 117½"

All fabrics at least 45" wide prewashed.
Fabric Requirements:
9 yds. background fabric
4 yds. pinwheel fabrics
½ inner border fabric
2 yds. outer border fabric

Directions:
1. Piece blocks and cut alternate plain blocks as in small *Ribbon Pinwheel* quilt above. You will need 176 of each. Make four quilt sections as in the diagram at right.

2. Sew two sections together vertically as shown. Sew the other two together vertically. Turn one pair of sections upside down and seam both pairs together. Add a 1½" inner border and a 6" outer border.

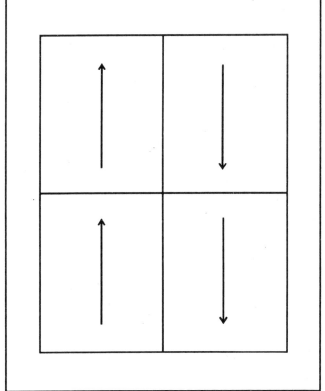

UMBRELLA

6" triangle
Quilt with border: 48¼" x 57½"

All fabrics at least 45" wide prewashed.
Fabric Requirements:
12 selvage to selvage 6¾" strips of
preshrunk fabric
      or:
2½ yds. total fabric (If particular patterns
are being cut from the fabric, more yardage
will be required.)
1¼ yds. border fabric

Directions:
1. Cut 100 teardrop shapes from 6¾" strips
of fabric.

Teardrop

2. Arrange the teardrops on a floor or wall
to produce the pattern or effect desired.
Then pick up sets of three teardrops to
produce the umbrella block.

3. Sew two teardrops together (a), then set
in the third teardrop (b&c).

This is a complete *Umbrella* block. Make 30
of these.

TIP Begin sewing at the edge and seam
down to the center. Stop at the seam
allowance (some people mark this with a
dot, or you can learn to estimate it), and
backstitch. Take out of the sewing machine
and do another set of two.

a)
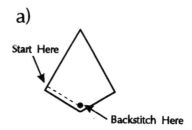

To set in the third teardrop sew from the
edge to the center seam allowance and
backstitch, flipping the bulk of the
underneath seam out of the way. Take out
from under the needle and line up the final
seam, flipping the bulk of the back seam in
the opposite direction. Begin stitching in the
center, taking one backstitch and then
stitching out to the edge. When you press,
gently lay the seams in the direction they
wish to go.

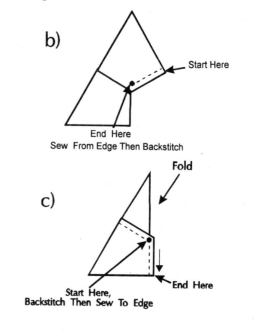

Umbrella

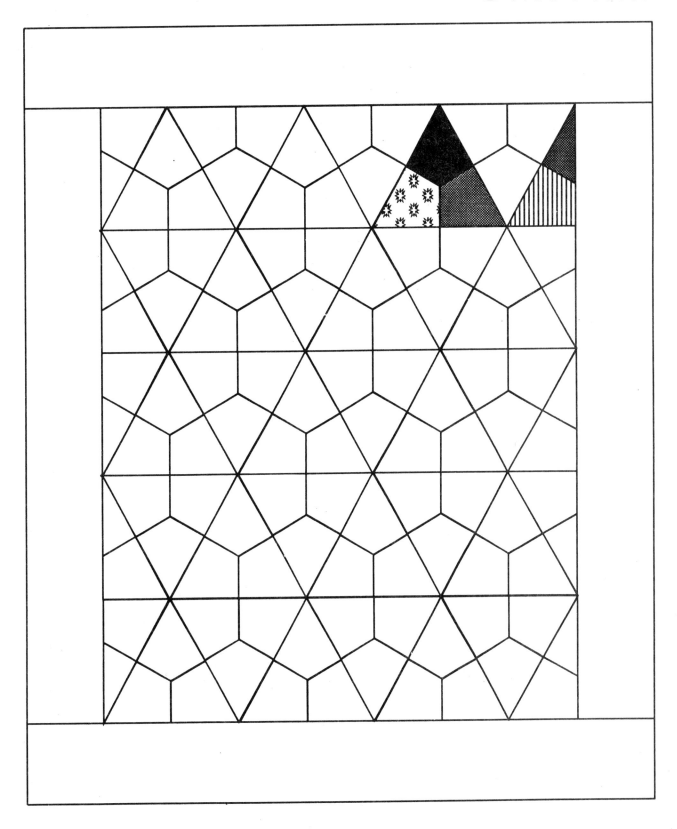

4. Sew six *Umbrella* blocks into a horizontal row. Cut five 6½" triangles and bisect them to produce 6½" triangle halves. Sew onto teardrops as shown to produce six left and six right fill-in pieces. Finish the left and right ends of each row with the needed finishing piece. Make five rows altogether.

Fill-in Pieces

5. Sew the rows together and add a 6" border.

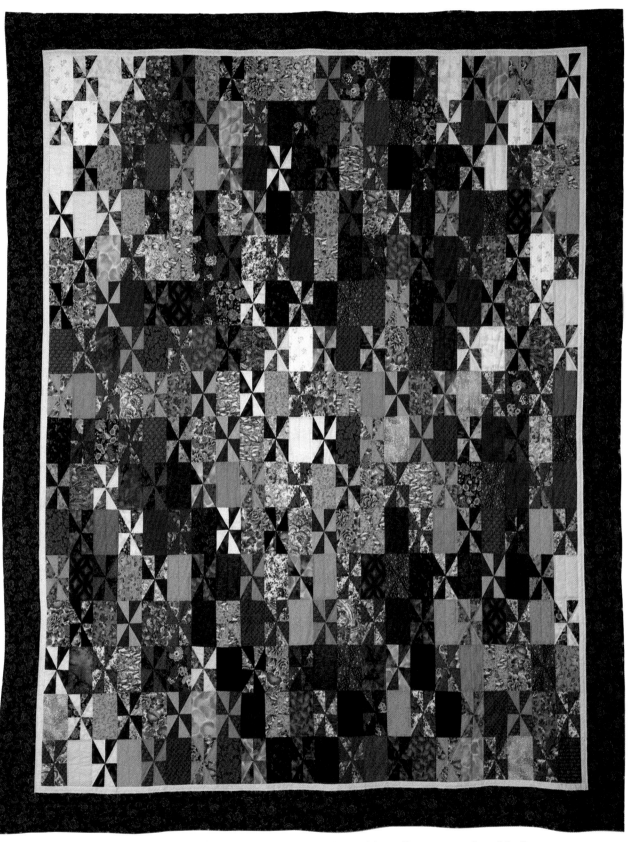

Ribbon Pinwheel, 96" x 117½". A landscape of color. This quilt top was pieced in four sections, each a complete design in itself, and then these were combined into one grand design. Texture and color blend and separate as the eye travels over the surface. Pieced by Marjorie Lorant and quilted by Pat Beck.

Diamond Rain, 67½" x 84". The stripes and plaids in this strip-pieced quilt add so much direction and motion to the design that the diamonds seem to vibrate and blur. Brilliant reds and yellows add even more impact. Quilted by Penny Wolf.

Cough Drop, 42" x 48". A novelty print is the inspiration for a special technique used in piecing this quilt. A small printed person is surrounded by crazy log-cabin pieces, in a mix of colors and prints. Then the long hex shape is cut from this newly constructed fabric. Some of the long hexes are cut from plain fabric. An unusual color scheme is set off by the perfect border fabric. Pieced by Betty Parks.

Old-Fashioned Diamond, 68" x 77½". the consistent arrangement of light and dark fabrics in each quilt block causes long twisted streamers to appear down the surface of the design. Fabrics with a hand dyed look add texture and a modern mood. Pieced by Bonnie Mitchell. Bonnie followed the suggestion on pg. 26 to make a larger quilt from the Old-Fashioned Diamond pattern.

Lotus, 49" x 59". This quilt looks like a colorful garden seen through the eyes of a child. A dark brown background was the warm starting point for these vibrant hues. Some cotton satin adds a soft shine here and there.

Umbrella, 48¼" x 57½". Another special collection of fabrics is combined in this exciting design. Ikot, shibori, marbleized fabrics, a bargello print, and border stripes were chosen and carefully cut and placed. This creates new patterns, starfish or snowflakes, propellers or flowers, depending on your imagination. An overdyed white-on-white print makes a special border. Quilted by Beverly Payne.

Lightning Bolt, 48¼" x 60". A "striking" quilt with an Amish look. Reverse placement of values adds contrast at top and bottom and blends the rows together in the center. At no place in the quilt are seams required to match, since it is lined up along the edges. Quilted by Nadine Darby.

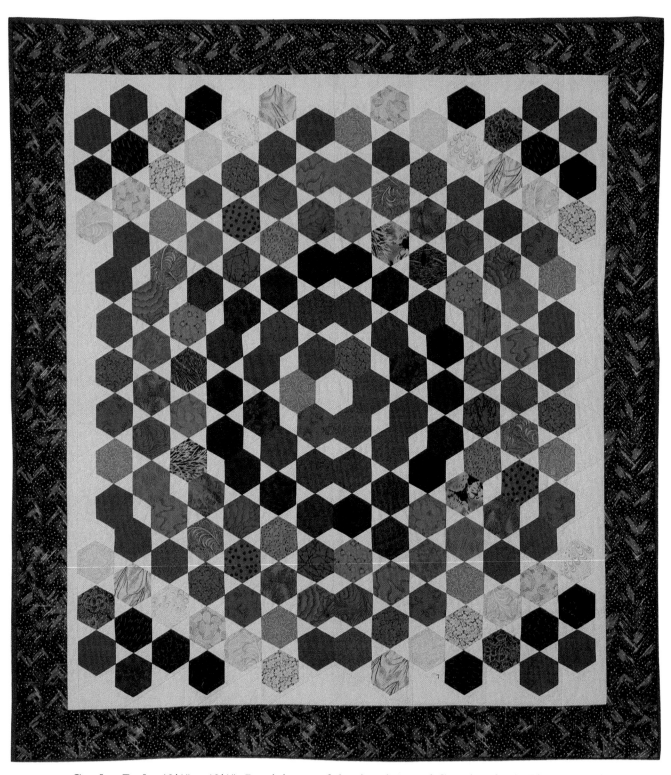

Garden Path, 43½" x 48½". Reminiscent of the time-honored Grandmother's Flower Garden quilts, this pattern has all straight seams. Radiating circles of color end with a cluster of hexagons on each corner. A happy baby quilt. Pieced by Kathleen Springer and quilted by Penny Wolf.

FACETS

4" triangle size
Quilt with borders: 25½" x 28¾"

All fabrics at least 45" wide prewashed.
Fabric Requirements:
9 strips--three light, three medium, three dark--cut 2⅜" wide
4½" strip of background fabric (or scraps)
¼ yd. inner border fabric
⅓ yd. outer border fabric

Directions:

1. Cut nine selvage to selvage 2⅜" strips of fabric. Cut 68 diamond halves from these strips.

2. Sew two half-diamonds together (a), then set in the third half-diamond (b&c).

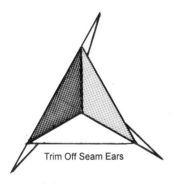
Trim Off Seam Ears

This is a complete *Facets* block. Make 20 of these, using assorted colors.

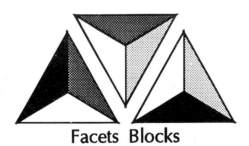
Facets Blocks

TIP Begin sewing at the edge of the narrow point and sew the seam down to the wider point. Stop at the seam allowance (some people mark this with a dot, or you can learn to estimate it) and backstitch. Take out of the sewing machine and do another set of two.

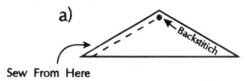
a)
Sew From Here
Backstitch

To set in the third diamond half sew from the point to the seam allowance and backstitch, flipping the bulk of the underneath seam out of the way. Take out from under needle and line up the final seam, flipping the bulk of the back seam in the opposite direction. Begin stitching in the center, taking one backstitch and then stitching out across the narrow points. When you press, gently lay the seams in the direction they wish to go.

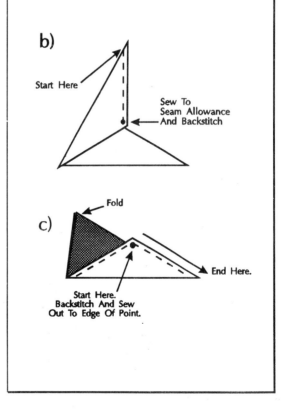
b)
Start Here
Sew To Seam Allowance And Backstitch

c)
Fold
Start Here. Backstitch And Sew Out To Edge Of Point.
End Here.

4. Cut eight triangle halves from 4½" triangles, using assorted colors. Using one triangle half and one diamond half, make four left finishing pieces and four right finishing pieces.

5. Using two finishing pieces and five complete blocks, sew a horizontal row. Make four rows. Sew the rows together. Add a 1¼" inner border and a 2½" outer border.

Note: To reduce bulk and help to line up all the points at seam intersections, press and sew so that the little seam triangles stick out along the edge of each row.

Finishing Pieces

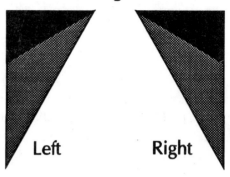

Left   Right

Horizontal Row of Facets

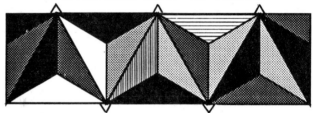

Facets

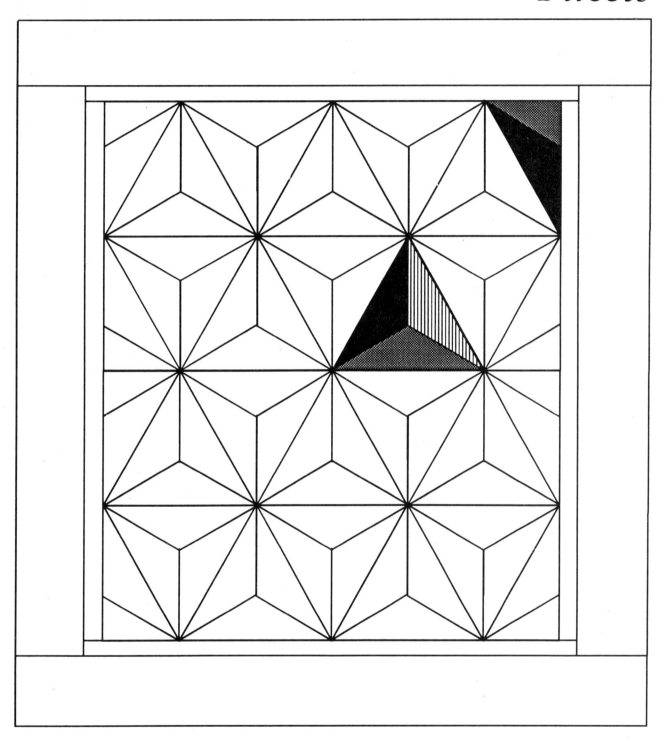

DIAMOND RAIN

4" triangle size
Quilt with border: 67½" x 84"

All fabrics at least 45" wide prewashed.
Fabric Requirements:
3¾ yds. of assorted fabrics
⅓ yd. background fabric
2 yds. border fabric

Directions:

1. Cut thirty-two 3¾" strips. Lay one side of the Clearview Triangle along the edge of each strip at one end and trim to a 60° angle. Sew four strips together lengthwise, lining up the angled ends as shown. Make seven more sets of strips like this.

2. Check angle at end of strip, and then cut 3¾" widths from each set of strips, checking the angle occasionally. You will need 64 of these units altogether.

3. Sew four strip widths into one block as shown. Separate and resew diamond sections to control color placement. Make 16 blocks.

4. Cut eight 7¾" x 4½" rectangles of background fabric. Lay rectangles right sides up and cut diagonally as shown. From two diamonds and two triangle halves make a finishing piece as shown. Sew four blocks and two finishing pieces into a vertical row. Make four rows. Sew the rows together and add an 8" border.

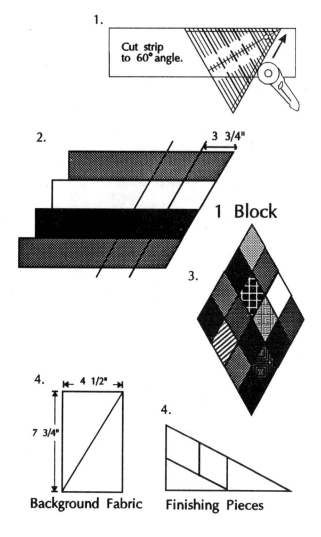

1. Cut strip to 60° angle.

2.   3 3/4"

1 Block

3.

4. 4 1/2"   7 3/4"   Background Fabric

4. Finishing Pieces

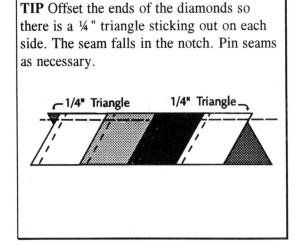

TIP Offset the ends of the diamonds so there is a ¼" triangle sticking out on each side. The seam falls in the notch. Pin seams as necessary.

1/4" Triangle   1/4" Triangle

Diamond Rain

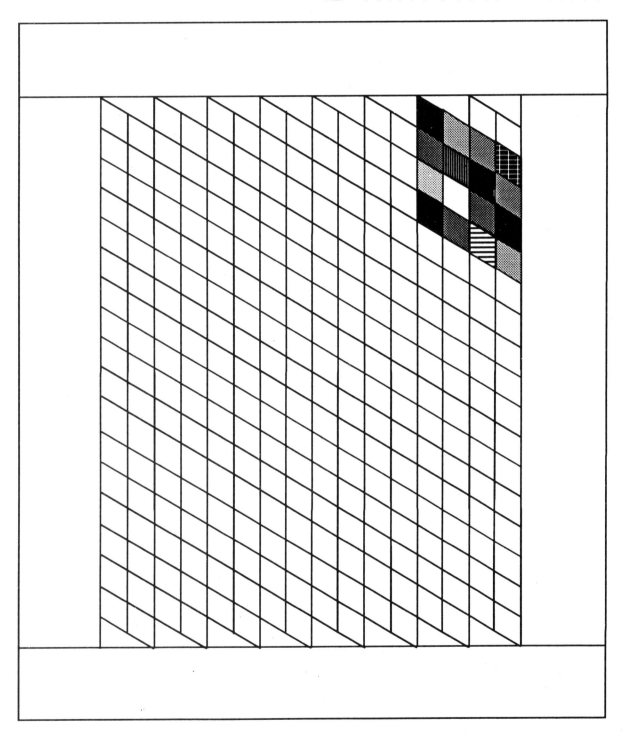

LIGHTNING BOLT

4" triangle size
Quilt with border: 48¼" x 60"

All fabrics at least 45" wide prewashed.
Fabric Requirements:
24 strips of fabric 3¾" wide (choose six colors, each color in four values)
5" strip of background fabric
1¼ yds. of border fabric

Directions:
1. Decide which colors will be the outside rows. Set those eight fabrics aside. From the remaining fabrics cut 48 long diamonds from a 3¾" strip at 7" on the Clearview Triangle. Cut four of each color. *(Note: The long diamond does have a reverse of its shape. If you are working with solids you can simply flip them over, otherwise, check to be sure you are cutting the points of the long diamonds in the right direction.)* Arrange in four vertical rows, having each row consist of one color from light to dark. Reverse the value range in alternate rows. Sew the long diamonds into diagonal rows of four. Press to the dark fabrics in each strip.

2. From the eight outside colors cut 24 flat pyramids from a 3¾" strip at 7¼" on the Clearview Triangle. Finish the diagonal rows at left and right with the flat pyramids. Finish the diagonal rows at the top and bottom with a background diamond half cut from a 2½" strip. Sew all the diagonal rows together. Pin the ends with the ¼" triangle sticking out, and then sew.

3. Finish the left top and right bottom corners with a finishing piece made from a flat pyramid, a background diamond half, and a background triangle half cut from a 2⅜" x 4½" rectangle as shown. Add a 6½" border.

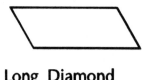
Long Diamond

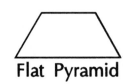
Flat Pyramid

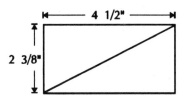
4 1/2"
2 3/8"

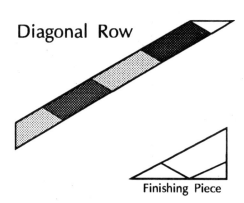
Diagonal Row

Finishing Piece

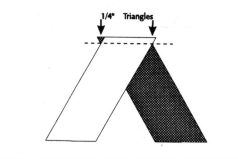
TIP Offset the short ends so a ¼" fabric triangle sticks out at either end. The seam falls in the notch.

1/4" Triangles

Lightning Bolt

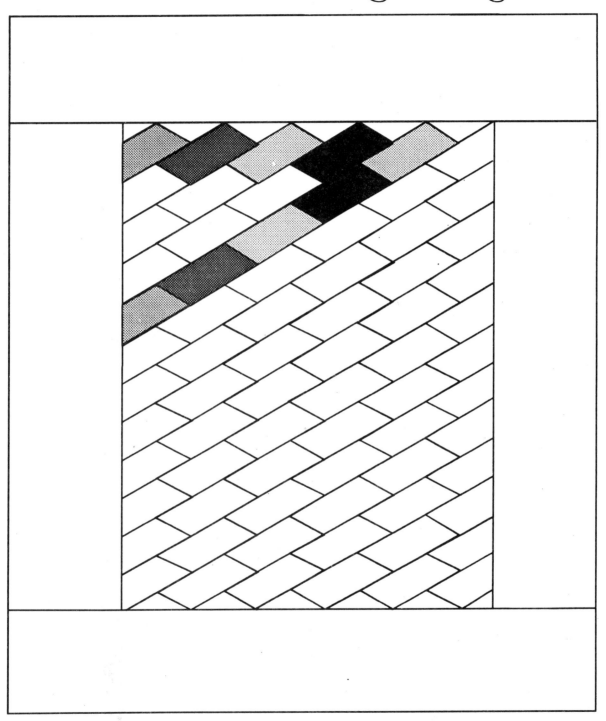

COUGH DROP

3" triangle size
Quilt with borders: 42" x 48"

All fabrics at least 45" wide prewashed.
Fabric Requirements:
⅓ yd. each of three long hex colors
¼ yd. each of four long hex colors
½ yd. background fabric
⅓ yd. inner border fabric
⅔ yd. outer border fabric

Directions:
1. Cut for one half-block:
1 long hex from a 5" strip of fabric at the
7¼" line on the Clearview Triangle. Cut a
long diamond, then cut a 2½" triangle off
both ends. (40 will be needed altogether)
2 background 3" triangles (72 will be
needed altogether).
Sew a triangle at either end of the long hex
as shown. Make 32 of these.

2. Make *Cough Drop* blocks by sewing two
half-blocks together as shown. Make 12
blocks altogether.

3. Cut eight background triangle halves
from four 2" x 3½" rectangles and four
4⅝" x 8" rectangles as shown.

4. Sew one 3" background triangle and one
3½" background triangle half to each of the
remaining eight long hexes. Combine these
with the remaining half-blocks and the 8"
background triangle halves to make eight top
and bottom finishing pieces.

5. Sew three *Cough Drop* blocks and two
finishing pieces into a vertical row as shown
in the quilt diagram. Make four rows
altogether. Sew the rows together. Add a 2"
inner border and a 4¾" outer border.

Cough Drop

Half Block

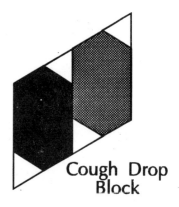
Cough Drop Block

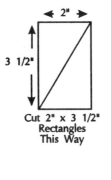

← 2" →
3 1/2"
Cut 2" x 3 1/2"
Rectangles
This Way

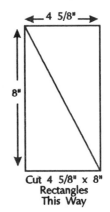

← 4 5/8" →
8"
Cut 4 5/8" x 8"
Rectangles
This Way

Last 8 Long Hexes

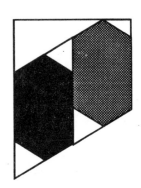
Finishing Block

Cough Drop

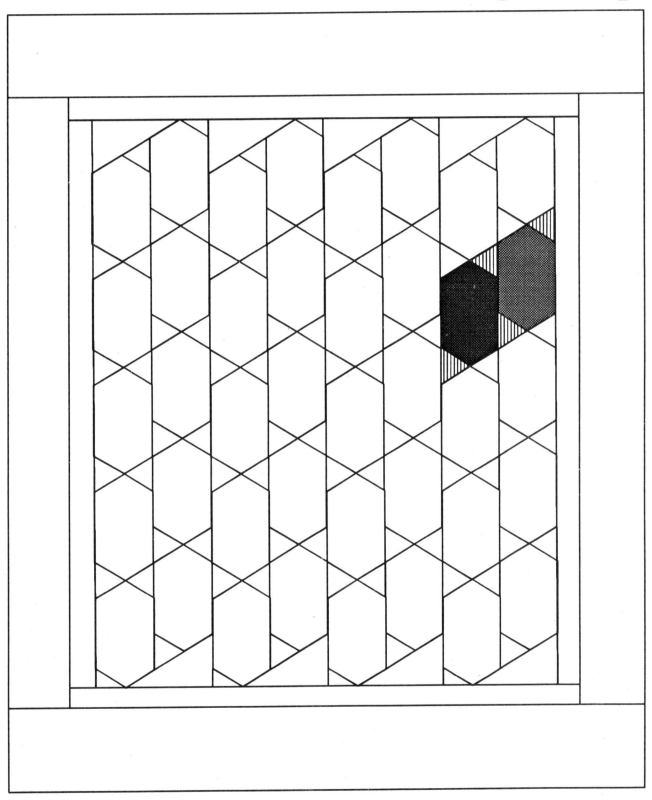

LOTUS

2" triangle size
Quilt with border: 49" x 59"

All fabrics at least 45" wide prewashed.
Fabric Requirements:
⅓ yd. each of eight or more flower colors
1½ yds. background fabric
1¼ yds. border fabric

Directions:
1. Cut for one block:
6 gem shapes from a 3" strip
4 background 2" triangles from a 2" strip
4 background diamonds from a 1¾" strip

2. Sew three gem shapes together from center to seam allowance and backstitch. Set two background diamonds in the two notches on the outside edge.
Sew a 2" triangle on each outside corner.
Make two half-blocks in the same color. DO NOT SEAM THESE TOGETHER NOW.
Make 70 half-blocks altogether.

3. Sew seven half-blocks in a row, turning them alternately to the left and the right. Sew another row of seven, turning the half-blocks to match the first row and complete four blocks, including the top and bottom blocks. Finish the top and bottom of each row with a 5" triangle half cut from a 5" triangle. Sew these two rows together.

Top ◄——— Vertical Row Of 7 Half-blocks

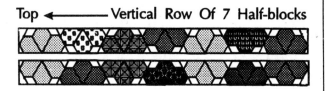

4. Make five complete double sets of *Lotus* rows altogether. Sew the rows together and add a 6" border.

Gem Shape

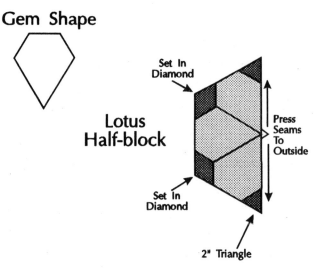

Lotus Half-block

Set In Diamond

Press Seams To Outside

Set In Diamond

2" Triangle

TIP To set in the background diamond: sew from the outside edges to the seam allowance and backstitch, flipping the bulk of the underneath seam out of the way. Take out from under needle and line up the final seam, flipping the bulk of the back seam in the opposite direction. Begin stitching in the center, taking one backstitch and then stitching out to the edge. Press the seams gently in the direction they wish to go.

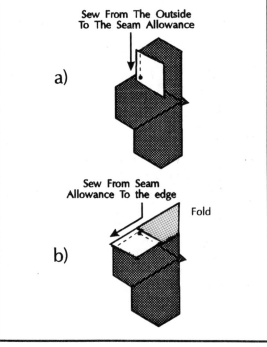

Sew From The Outside To The Seam Allowance

a)

Sew From Seam Allowance To the edge

Fold

b)

Lotus

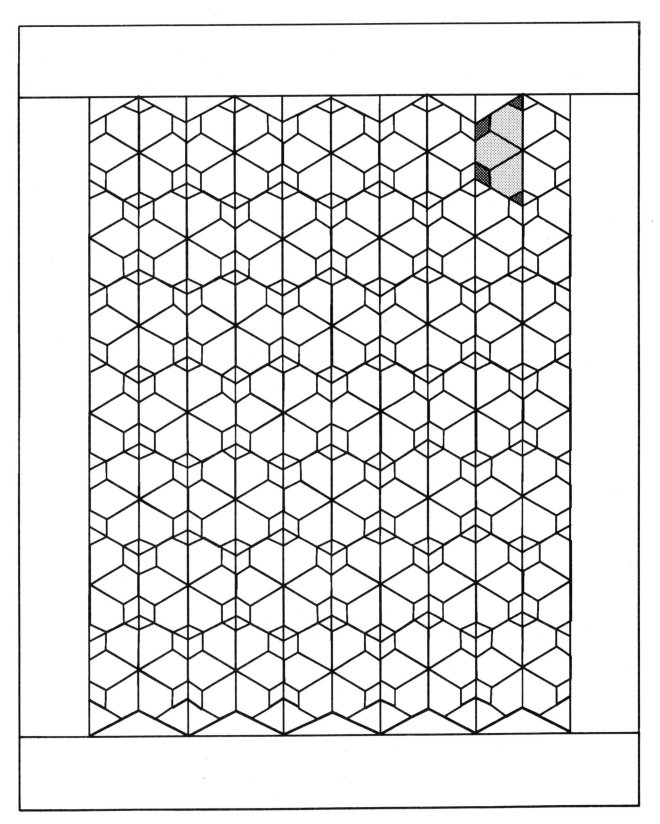

GARDEN PATH

2" triangle size
Quilt with borders: 43½" x 48½"

All fabrics at least 45" wide prewashed.
Fabric Requirements:
6 hexagons - red-orange
20 hexagons - fuschia
18 hexagons - purple
24 hexagons - turquoise
30 hexagons - lavender
36 hexagons - scarlet
24 hexagons - peach
16 hexagons - blue

One 3" prewashed strip of red-orange
¼ yd. of fuschia
¼ yd. of purple
½ yd. of turquoise
½ yd. of lavender
½ yd. of scarlet
½ yd. of peach
¼ yd. of blue
1 yd. background fabric
1/3 yd. border fabric

Directions:
1. Cut hexagons from 3" strips of fabric.
Cut a 60° diamond first, then cut a 1½"
triangle off each end to produce the
hexagon. Cut the number of hexagons from
each color as shown above.

2. Cut 168 background 2" triangles from a
2" strip. Also cut six 2" triangles from
typing paper or the equivalent. Sew two
background 2" triangles to each hexagon as
shown except to the six center red-orange
hexagons. Sew one 2" paper triangle and
one 2" fabric triangle to each center red-
orange hexagon. Press to the triangle.

3. Cut 14 background 3¼" triangles.
Assemble the left and right side wedges in
rows as shown, ending each row at the
outside with a 3¼" background triangle.
The paper triangle should be at the center.
Follow color order carefully.

Hexagon

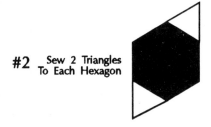

#2 Sew 2 Triangles
To Each Hexagon

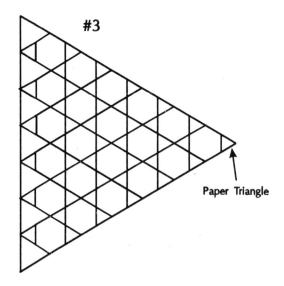

#3

Paper Triangle

Garden Path

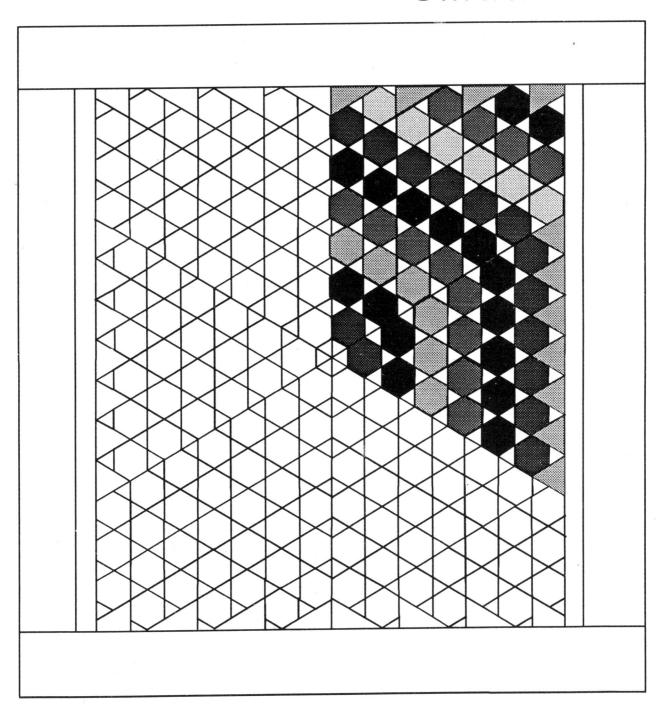

4. Cut eight background 6¼" triangles. Bisect to produce left and right background triangle halves.

5. Assemble two left and two right corner wedges as shown. Assemble in two-row sets, finishing the top of each pair of rows with a 6¼" background triangle half. The paper triangle should be at the center of the quilt. The background triangle half will extend past the quilt edge at the left and right side. Trim even with the side of the quilt.

6. Sew the wedges into a left set of three and a right set of three. Then sew the two halves of the quilt together.

7. Rotary cut one hexagon from background fabric as above. Rotary cut a paper hexagon from a 2½" strip of paper. (Cut a diamond, then cut off a 1¼" triangle from each end.) Baste the fabric hex over the paper hex, turning the edges under. Then appliqué the paper-pieced background hexagon over the seamed center paper triangles. Remove ALL the papers from behind, snipping threads carefully as necessary. Press the quilt top. Seam a 1¼"strip of background fabric at left and right. Add a 4" final border.

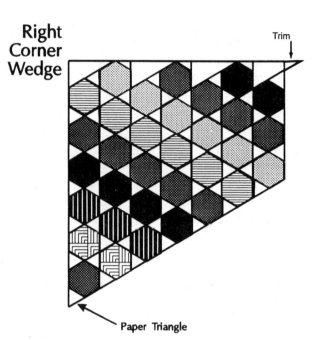

Right Corner Wedge

Trim

Paper Triangle

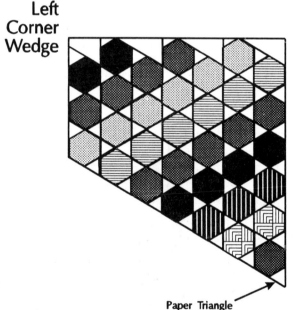

Left Corner Wedge

Paper Triangle

Bibliography

Benberry, Cuesta. *Charm Quilts Revisited*.
Quilters Newsletter Magazine #198, pgs. 30-35.

Beyers, Jinny. *The Scrap Look*. McLean, VA: EPM
Publishers, Inc., 1985.

Brackman, Barbara. *Clues in the Calico*. McLean,
VA, EPM Publications, Inc., 1989.

Brackman, Barbara. *An Encyclopedia of Pieced Quilt
Patterns, Vol. 1*. Laurence, KS, Prairie Flower
Publishing, 1979.

Morse, J.L. *Funk & Wagnalls New Encyclopedia*.
New York, Funk & Wangalls, Inc., 1972.

Index of Cutting Directions

About the Author

Sara Nephew began her artistry in metalwork. After receiving her B.A. as an Art Major, she worked for a commercial shop, designing and repairing jewelry, and invented a new enamel-on-brass technique. Her cloisonné work appeared in national exhibits.

She has since turned her interests to quilting, in large part because of the many attractions of fabric. Sara is the originator of a series of tools for rotary cutting isometric shapes, and is a nationally known teacher.

Sara is the author of five previous quilting books. *Quilts From a Different Angle* was an introduction to 60° triangle quilts. *My Mother's Quilts: Designs From the Thirties* helped inspire renewed interest in Depression-era quilts. *Stars and Flowers: Three-sided Patchwork* showed how to speed-piece 60° quilts with a floral appliqué appearance. And her fourth and fifth books, *Building Block Quilts*, and *Building Block Quilts 2*, explored isometric 3-D illusions. With three friends, Sara also co-authored a book on rotary cutting triangle quilts, *Quick and Easy Quiltmaking.*

Sara lives in Snohomish, Washington, with her husband Dale, and their three children.

Available from Clearview Triangle

60° 6" Clearview Triangle - ruled every 1/4"	$6.50 plus $1.50 shipping*
60° 12" Clearview Triangle - ruled every 1/4"	$11.50 plus $2.00 shipping*
60° 8" Mini-Pro - ruled every 1/8"	$9.50 plus $1.75 shipping*
120° Half-Diamond - ruled every 1/8"	$10.50 plus $2.00 shipping*
2-sided graph paper pad - 30 sheets	$5.95 plus $1.00 shipping*
Stars and Flowers: Three-sided Patchwork	$12.95 plus $2.00 shipping*
Building Block Quilts	$14.95 plus $2.00 shipping*
Building Block Quilts 2	$14.95 plus $2.00 shipping*

* *Subtract $1.00 from shipping for each item after the first.*

Order From: Clearview Triangle
Dept. 4
8311 180th St. S.E.
Snohomish, WA 98290
USA